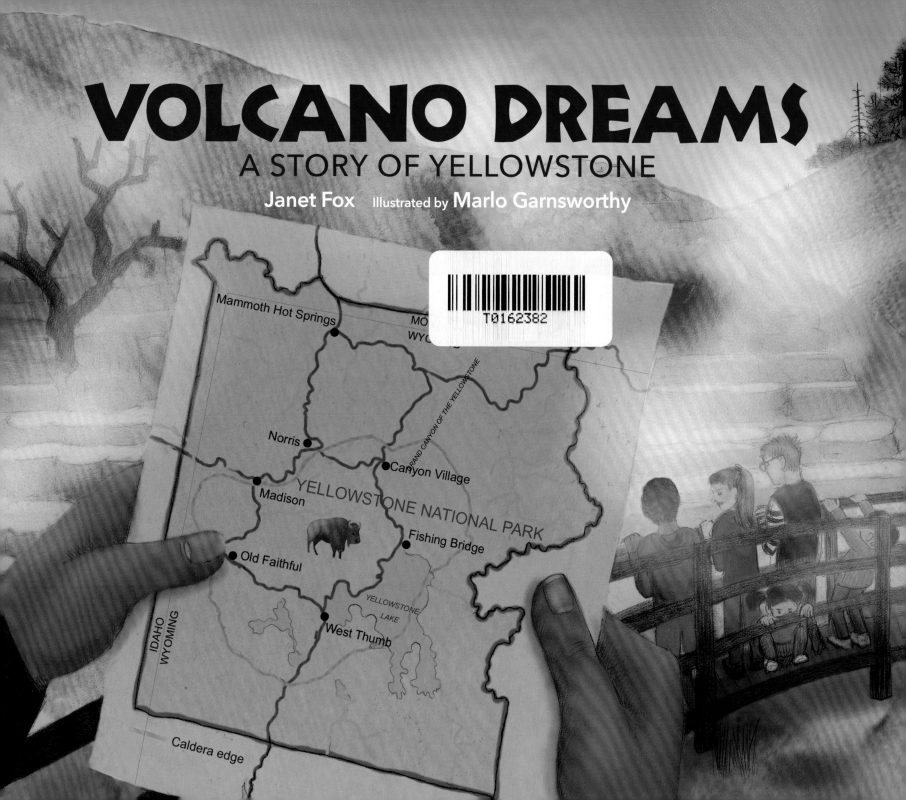

VOLCANO DREAMS

A STORY OF YELLOWSTONE

Janet Fox   Illustrated by **Marlo Garnsworthy**

Mammoth Hot Springs

MO
WYO

Norris

GRAND CANYON OF THE YELLOWSTONE

Canyon Village

YELLOWSTONE NATIONAL PARK

Madison

Old Faithful

Fishing Bridge

YELLOWSTONE LAKE

West Thumb

IDAHO
WYOMING

Caldera edge

As the sun rises, something is sleeping in Yellowstone.

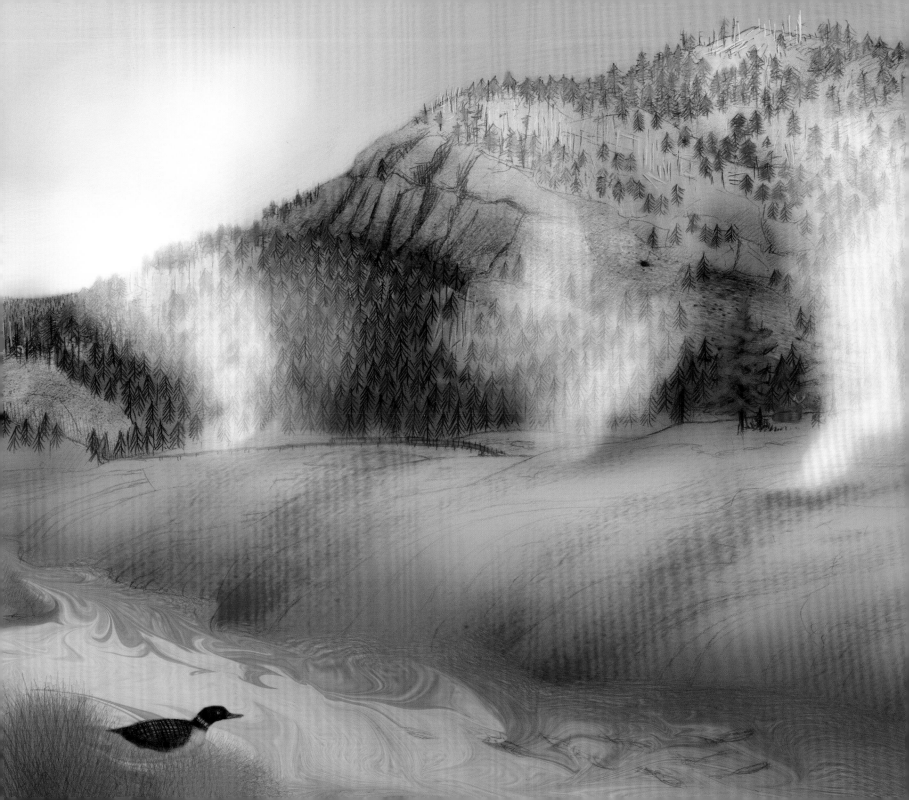

The wolf isn't sleeping.
She opens her watchful blue eyes while her pups nurse.

The moose isn't sleeping.
He wades into the murky water and scoops up wads of pondweed.

The bear isn't sleeping.
She strips chokecherries from a branch with her sharp-clawed paws.

Is the elk sleeping?
No, he lifts his antlered head and bugles across the aspen-gold meadow.

Is the big horn ram sleeping?
No. He tilts his head and crashes—boom!—against his brother.

Is the mountain goat sleeping?

No. She dances up the sheer cliff on her flexing feet.

The grazing buffalo grumble and grunt, wide awake.

The mountain lion peers through the branches, ever watchful.
The coyote howls, his song echoing.

Even the earth isn't sleeping in Yellowstone.

Mud pots bubble and burp.

Steam vents hiss and gurgle.

Geysers spout and roar.

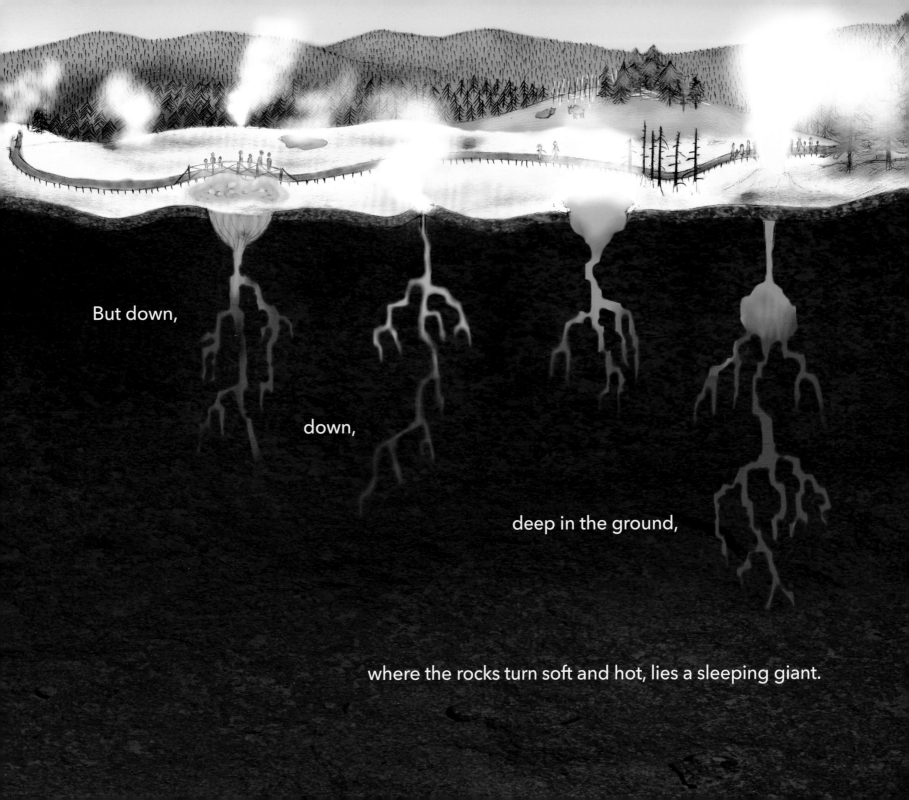

But down,

down,

deep in the ground,

where the rocks turn soft and hot, lies a sleeping giant.

A great volcano dreams beneath the earth's surface.
Fiery **magma** forms the giant's heart.

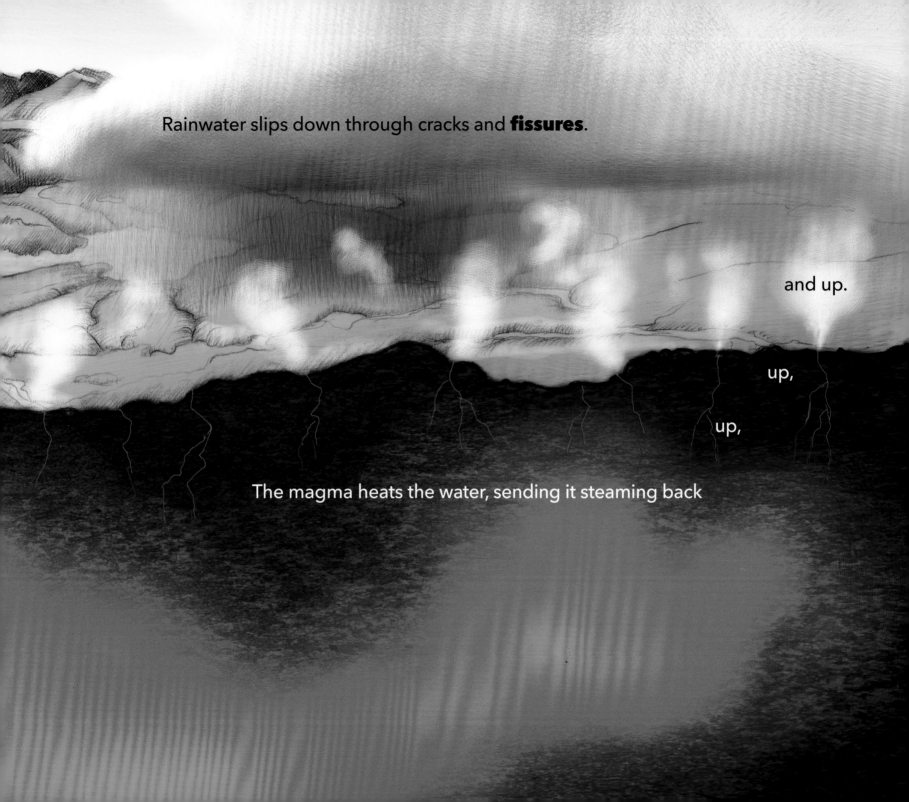

Rainwater slips down through cracks and **fissures**.

and up.

up,

up,

The magma heats the water, sending it steaming back

Ages upon ages ago, the giant stirred awake.
The mountains stretched and yawned and rolled like thunder.

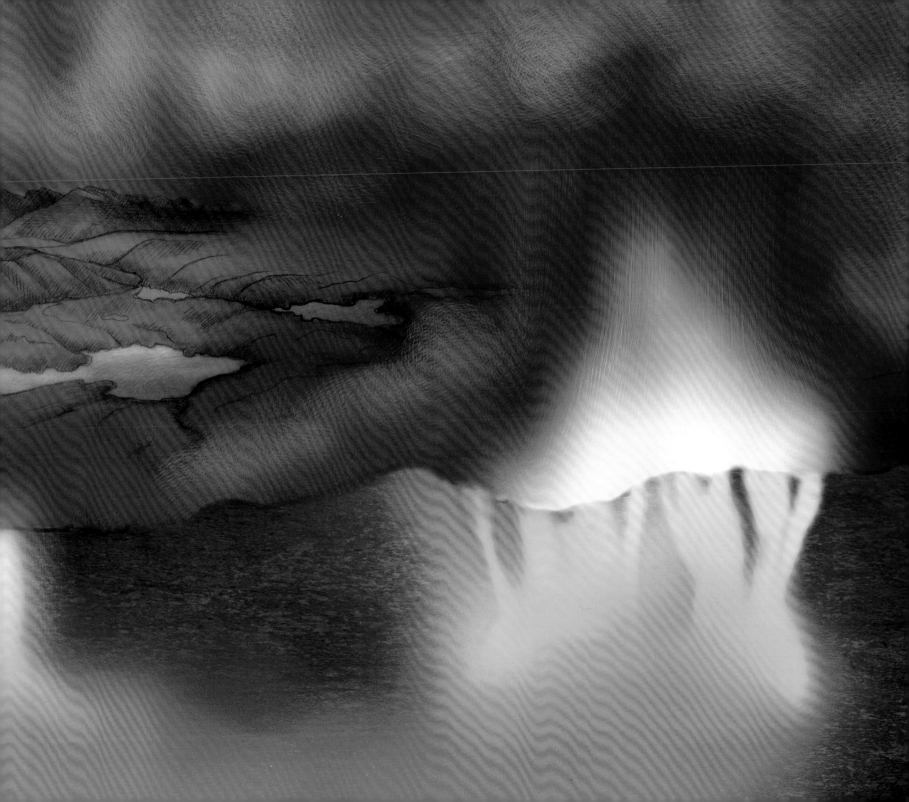

Steam vents shrieked.

Geysers thrust their watery fists into the sky.

Mud pots roiled like cauldrons.

The giant shrugged aside its heavy cover...

and its magma heart poured out,
cooling into rocks.

Volcanic ash and **pumice** formed great yellow cliffs.

Lava chilled in tall columns, creating **columnar joints**.

Liquid rock froze into black **obsidian** glass.

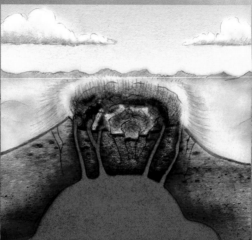 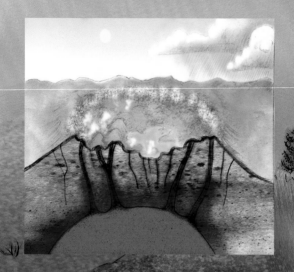

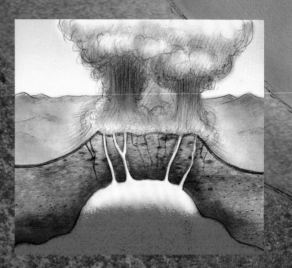

When the giant grew weary, it fell back to drowsy sleep. The cooling earth above collapsed

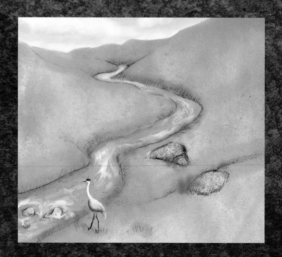  

and left **caldera** edges to be carved by streams and rivers into deep canyons.

Seedlings sprouted in the fertile ash and made pine forests and wildflowered hills.

Now the giant rests, slumbering through molten time, wrestling with its volcano dreams. The years may number tens of thousands before it wakes again.

But today, the animals find refuge near **hot springs** and in lush meadows.
They find shelter under cool pines and inside yellow caves.

The elk tucks his bulk into feathered grass.

The bear curls her body inside her earthen den.

The mother wolf nestles her head over her deep-breathing pups.

And the volcano dreams beneath them all as the sun sets.

GLOSSARY

A **caldera** is a large crater-like depression that is created when an emptied volcano collapses in on itself after erupting.

Columnar joints are formed when, as lava cools, the resulting rock fractures into regular polygonal columns.

A **fissure** is a long, narrow, deep crack.

Geysers eject fountains of hot water and steam high into the air. Geysers are formed when rainwater seeps into the earth and is heated to boiling before returning to the surface explosively.

Hot springs are places where the superheated water exits the rock through a large fissure or a funnel-shaped hole.

Lava is magma that has erupted from a volcano.

Magma is hot liquid rock deep under the earth's surface.

Mud pots are boiling ponds made of mud that bubbles and spatters.

Obsidian is a glassy, black volcanic rock formed from lava that cools rapidly during an eruption.

Pumice is a light and porous rock with a gritty texture; pumice forms when gas-rich lava cools quickly and gas bubbles are trapped in the forming rock.

Steam vents form when rainwater is superheated by hot rocks deep beneath the earth and then rises—like steam from a teakettle—through thin cracks in the rocks.

Volcanic ash is made up of small dust-like particles that blow out of a volcano during an eruption and blanket the earth for miles around, mixing with soil and providing rich nutrients to plants.

MORE ABOUT YELLOWSTONE AND ITS VOLCANO

Yellowstone National Park is the United States' first national park, established in 1872. The Park spreads across parts of three states—Wyoming, Montana, and Idaho—and is home to the many wild animals depicted in this book, as well as thousands of thermal features like geysers and hot springs.

The thermal features are there because Yellowstone is actually an immense volcano—even though it does not have the cone-shaped mountain we usually associate with volcanoes. All we can see of the volcano are its thermal features and caldera, but deep beneath the Park is a huge magma chamber. When the Yellowstone volcano erupts it is so large and explosive that we call it a "supervolcano." The Yellowstone supervolcano is now dormant (currently inactive). The most recent eruption of the Yellowstone supervolcano happened about 640,000 years ago, and the 1,500-square-mile (2,414-square-kilometer) Yellowstone caldera was formed when the volcano collapsed. (The map on the title page shows where the edges of the Yellowstone caldera are.)

The mud pots, hot springs, geysers, and steam vents in the Park are made by rainwater that is superheated by the Yellowstone magma chamber. Algae that live in the hot springs and geysers create brilliant colors. Geysers like the reliable Old Faithful can shoot thousands of gallons of water to up to hundreds of feet in the air with each eruption.

Because of its fertile volcanic ash soil, Yellowstone is lush with trees like quaking aspen and brilliant wildflowers like paintbrush. The animals that roam the Park are protected and, in the winter, tend to gather near the thermal features to keep warm. The Park is open year-round to visitors who come from all over the world to see this beautiful wonderland.

To Kevin and Jeff, my geyser-gazers.
—J.F.

To Mutti, lifting me high, & Scott, ever standing by.
—M.G.

Text © 2018 by Janet Fox.
Illustrations © 2018 by Marlo Garnsworthy.

For ages 5-9

All rights reserved. No part of this book may be reproduced or utilized in any form or by any means, electronic or mechanical, including photocopying, recording, or any information storage in a retrieval system, without permission in writing from the publisher.

Published in the United States in 2018 by Web of Life Children's Books, Berkeley, California. Second printing 2021.

Library of Congress Control Number: 2017960443

ISBN 978-0-9883303-9-9

The artwork for this book was prepared using graphite on paper, watercolor collage, and digital oil.

For free, downloadable activities, and for more information about our books and the authors and artists who created them, visit our website:
www.weboflifebooks.com

Distributed by Publishers Group West/An Ingram Brand
(800) 788-3123

FSC
MIX
Paper from
responsible sources